Great Americana

A Journal
of the Overland Route to California

Lorenzo D. Aldrich

A Journal
of the Overland Route
to California

by Lorenzo D. Aldrich

READEX MICROPRINT

Foreword

Most of the accounts of the early overland trips across
the American continent after the discovery of gold in California describe the middle route, usually with St. Louis
or one of the towns in that area as the staging point for
the journey westward. Lorenzo D. Aldrich's *A Journal of
the Overland Route to California*, a very rare tract, de-
scribes the southern route from Fort Smith, Arkansas, to
San Diego, California. It is one of the earliest reports of
this route.

Aldrich's *Journal* was published in 1851 at Lansingburgh, New York, his home town. An unsigned introduc-
tion, probably by the local printer, reported Aldrich's
death and suggests that he did not meet with success in
his search for gold in California. The editor, however,
hopes that though he failed to find proper recompense
here below, he has been "admitted to that 'upper sphere'"
where he now has "his reward." The conclusion of the
Journal has a note indicating that Aldrich contracted
malaria on the journey across the Isthmus of Panama on
his return from California and died soon after his arrival
at Lansingburgh.

The *Journal* begins on April 18 without indicating the
year, but the date is evidently 1848. It ends abruptly with
an entry in Panama on December 23, again without a year
date, but internal evidence suggests that the date is 1850.
The editor of the *Journal* apologizes for gaps in the manuscript and illegibility and mutilations. He has also deleted
portions: "Lest he [the author] should have been accused
of exaggerating, he [the editor] has withholden the recital

of hardships and sufferings, the publication of which would have swelled this pamphlet to double its present dimensions and invested it with harrowing interest."

The journey from Fort Smith was made by wagon and pack mule. Leaving Fort Smith on May 23, Aldrich's party made their way across Oklahoma, the Panhandle of Texas, along the Canadian River. They eventually arrived at Santa Fe and from there headed southwest toward Tucson, Arizona, following a trail that took them over difficult mountains and sandy deserts. Indians terrified them; rattlesnakes were a constant hazard; and quicksand in the rivers and sandstorms on the desert impeded them; but at last, on December 1, they reached San Diego, where they took a ship for San Francisco. At San Diego, Aldrich went to see a bullfight. "I saw nothing, however, that pleased me in the spectacle," he observes, "except the splendid horsemanship of the riders. Their skill in throwing the lance is admirable. The spectators appeared to be all highly delighted."

In San Francisco, Aldrich's group purchased a whaleboat and made the rest of the trip to the gold fields on the Yuba River by that form of transport. The *Journal* stops with their arrival at Yuba City, where, Aldrich notes, "Drinking and gambling are much practiced." It takes up again for three pages describing Aldrich's departure on the homeward journey via Panama. The importance of this brief diary is in its description of the southern route to California. For information about Aldrich's destination in California in this period, see Robert G. Cleland, *From Wilderness to Empire* (New York, 1944).

A Journal
of the Overland Route to California

A JOURNAL

OF

THE OVERLAND ROUTE

TO CALIFORNIA!

AND THE GOLD MINES,

BY
LORENZO D. ALDRICH,
LATE OF LANSINGBURGH, RENSSELAER CO. N. Y.

LANSINGBURGH, N. Y.
ALEXR. KIRKPATRICK, PRINTER; 265 STATE STREET
——1851.——

PREFACE.

In submitting the following pages to the eyes of the public, it might be well to premise that the author has studied to give a statement of *facts*, rather than to excite wonder by an overwrought or partially imaginative tale. He has dealt only in veritable incidents, without attempting to mislead by the interpolation of fictitious narative. Holding *truth* to be the only fitting guide to all valuable information, he has not sought to misrepresent the one by violating the other. Indeed there exists no necessity for having recourse to invention, or for throwing the mantle of romance over that which claims to be merely a plain "unvarnished" statement of facts.

The transcription of the manuscript, by reason of consideracle defacement—the frequent recurrence of *hiati*, and the occasional illegibility consequent on the hurry with which many portions of it must have been written, has been attended by no little difficulty, and the original subjected to much mutilation. It is believed, however, that the narrative will meet with full acceptance, and will be perused with no slight interest by the numerous friends of the author.

Lest he should have been accused of exaggerating, he has with-holden the recital of hardships and sufferings, the publication of which would have swelled this pamphlet to double its present dimensions, and have invested it with harrowing interest.

The memory of but few of our citizens will be cherished more fondly by the community at large, than that of L. D. Aldrich. Few who peruse this record of his hardships and distress, will fail to lament his mifortunes, and dwell regretfully on the melancholy issue of his enterprise.

Let the recollection of his public character and private virtue tend to assure our earnest hopes, and sustain us in the belief, that notwitstanding his arduous toil here below has failed in ensuring fitting recompense, he ere this inherits a far higher treasure than that of earth, and admitted to tl at " upper sphere," *has* "his reward."

DIARY OF THE OVERLAND ROUTE.

After taking leave half regretfully of the friends at Lansingburgh, I set out, accompanied by Alexander Stewart, James V. S. Stewart, Robert VanderCook, Alexander McDonald, Robert Blake, Cornelius F. VanderCar, J. W. Stewart, James Dutcher, William VanderCar, and N. N. Schouton; for that "aureate clime," the far off Land of California. Concerning the progress, character and issue of the enterprise, the reader will gather information, in the following pages.

APRIL 18th.   We left Albany at 1 o'clock this afternoon, in company with two parties from Boston, numbering all together about seventy.   Had rather an unpleasant journey as far as Rochester, at which place we did not arrive until about eleven o'clock the next day.   Took dinner there and went to see Genessee Falls which are quite a curiosity to such as have never seen any thing of this sort before.   Left Rochester at 1 o'clock for Buffalo, and arrived there about half past four in the evening—stopped at the Exchange Hotel, kept by T. C. Clinghorn, (which is nothing more than a second class tavern,) and remained there over one day for the purpose of visiting Niagara Falls, but were disappointed.   On going to the office of the cars and waiting until one in the afternoon, we received word through the agent that the locomotive had broken down on her return from the Falls, which intelligence was a source of great disappointment to all parties.   Stayed here until about four o'clock in the afternoon of Friday, and then took passage on board the steamboat America for Cleveland, Sandusky and Cincinatti—landed at Grand River, Cleveland. The latter place is a fine city, streets wider than any that I have ever seen in the New England States.   The Lake is as smooth as the North River is at the calmest time.   Everything is very agreeeable on board, the California Boys are all here and are enjoying themselves amazingly well in dancing. There had been nothing to mar the happy feelings of our company until the third engineer of the boat met with an accident terminating in his death.

Captain How and the officers on board are very agreeable companions, much more so than the generality of those on our

North River Boats. Arrived in Sandusky about four o'clock in the afternoon and took lodgings at the Exchange Hotel.

This city is, I should judge, rather on the decline. The buildings for the general part are old and in a dilapidated condition. Started for Cincinnatti at four o'clock on the evening of the 24th of April, arrived there about half past nine and put up at the Henry House for two or three days, employing this interval in laying in stores for the journey to California. We remained at Cincinnatti from Monday until Thursday evening—went to see the observatory and the telescope there, which is the largest in the United States.

I have seen nothing remarkable in the city except its dirty streets, smoky atmosphere and lean Hogs. Witnessed a sad accident to-day by reason of a load of dirt falling on a little boy of some five years old, killing him immediately. The cart was driven by the boy's father.

They have some of the finest horses here that I ever saw.

Leaving Cincinnatti, I proceeded down the Ohio River, on board the steamer *Bride*, (which is the only one I ever expect to sleep with,) for Louisville and Arkansas, distant about 900 miles from Cincinatti. Stopped a short time in Madison, Indianna, which is a small place, numbering about 600 inhabitants, and having a railroad to Indianapolis. Arrived at Louisville on the 27th and stayed over until the following day, two P. M., and then passed through the canal to Portland, which has three locks—visited Mr. Porter, the Kentucky giant, who is 6½ feet in height. Moved down one of the most pleasnt countries, made a few landings, and stopped at Cloverport on the Kentucky side. The bottom lands produce free, and the Bluffs limestone. Wherever you see a bluff on one side you will invariably perceive a bottom on the other. Stopped at Evensville, Indianna, and then reached the State of Illinois on the right, and passed the great cave, formerly frequented by Negro Stealers. Soon after we fell in with the steamer Bostonia which ran into the Bride and carried away her Jack staff, half severing her bows.

We have now been from Thursday the 26th of April until the present time, the 30th, accomplishing about 400 miles and are now lying perfectly still and have been so during the afternoon. The Ohio Steamers are the greatest impositions of any boats that I have ever travelled on, about equal in speed to our Troy tow-boats. We arrived at the mouth of the Ohio

at half past six o'clock A. M., on the 1st of May, stopped a-
bout an hour at Memphis and on the 2d reached Tenessee.—
The appearance of the city is more promising than I anticipat-
ed. It comprises a population of six or seven thousand, which
is increasing rapidly. The Navy Yard is of considerable
magnitude, occupying a number of buildings on the mouth of
Wolf River. Stopped at Hellena, Arkansas saw a small
bear and cubs, noticed a sign with the names of Baily & Rice
Merchants, inscribed upon it.

Arrived at Napoleon about 4 o'clock on the morning of the
3d, and took up our quarters on a wharf boat at six shillings
per day. There are some ten or fifteen buildings here—they
have neither Church nor School, and the state of society is
bad. They have a Courthouse but no Jail. We had green
Peas served up in a style that would try the stomach of a
Crocodile, and the most miserable fare that was ever set before man. There had been a great deal of Cholera and one
case terminating fatally on the day we left. We started for
Little Rock on May 4th, in the little screw Steamer Armstrong.
There was a twenty or thirty feet freshet when we went up
the river. The banks at the mouth are very low, timbered
principally with cotton wood, popple, and cane for under
brush. There are but few dwelling houses and these occur
at great distances from each other—saw a man grinding grain
with a hand mill. Sat. 5th,—fell in with a large flock of
wild Turkeys, Ducks and Geese. During the day saw a
number of plantations dotted with negro huts. The land
continued flat until we made Pine Bluff which is but an inconsiderable village. We arrived at Little Rock on Sunday
morning the 6th of May and put up at the Anthony House
a first rate establishment, where we found as good a table as
any we met on the road. This place is the only city in the
State and numbers about twenty five hundred inhabitants.—
Chester Ashly the late senator, deceased, was a resident of
this city. The State House here erected, is rather a fine
building, being composed of brick and coated with a plaster
having the appearance of marble. But little appears to be
done in the way of manufacture, most of the wares being im-
ported from abroad. They have an Arsenal, which can boast
of a few stand of Arms, and is rather a fine building. After
tarrying here three days we started for Fort Smith on board
the steamer Cotton Plant, Capt. Smith, at 11 o'clock A. M.

—stopped at different places on the way—arrived at the Fort at 1 o'clock, Friday, May 11th, and pitched our tent 1¼ miles from the village, remained here until Tuesday the 23rd, and then continued our rout with four mules and a four ox wagon. Traveled nine miles and stopped during the night on a prairie in the Choctaw Nation—took tea on raw ham and crackers, and started on Wednesday the 24th at 6 o'clock in the morning. Crossed the Porto river, a small stream about the size of the Erie canal and twenty five feet in depth.— Drove ten miles and halted for the night. Were visited by a number of Indians—thundered and rained till morning. May 25th, stopped over the day, fixed our harness, and cooked our provisions. Started on the morning of the 26th, about 7 o'clock—roads muddy and very wet—traveled eight miles through the worst road I ever saw—Mr. Osborn broke an axeltree and killed a rattlesnake. Put up for the night on a prairie, and lost two of our oxen which ran away, thus detaining us over a day. On the 27th of May, killed a rattlesnake under one of the wagons, found the oxen next morning, Sunday the 28th drove eight miles and halted. Sick all night with the chilling fever. Monday morning the 29th, started at 6⅔ o'clock, with faint hearts and empty stomachs, in consequence of the night's sickness, traveled about three miles, passing a few Indian huts. Our wagon in going over a small stream, broke down—shattering every spoke in one of the wheels—made about seven miles and put up. Repaired the wagon and laid over until 4½ on the 29th—then started and traveled 6 miles and halted for the night. May 30th, traveled 12 miles on a ridge road in the Choctaw Nation, and crossed the Law-Bay River—put up at two o'clock to repair Mr. Osborn's axeltree, and staid over until the next day.— Thunder and heavy rain throughout the night. May 31st started at 8 o'clock in the morning—very wet and muddy by reason of the rain during the night, traveled five miles and rested for dinner on the bank of Cooper's river, a small stream easily forded except during a freshet. Drove on in the afternoon and crossed little Sanboy river—traversed a large prairie, enriched by beautiful scenery and a range of mountains crowned with pine. Passed on for 10 miles over one of the worst mountains and rocks that can be imagned, and put up on a prairie over night. June 1st—Started at 7¼ o'clock and traveled through a low bottomed prairie—roads rough and

muddy, intersected by a ravine and some steep acclivities.
Mr. Stewart this afternoon broke the pole of his wagon—we
crossed a rough mountain at night and halted till morning on
a prairie. Traveled fifteen miles. June 2d—Started at 7½
o'clock A. M., drove one mile and crossed the south fork of
the Canadian river or Ganes creek, which took us until 2¼
o'clock in the afternoon the banks being very steep and difficult for trains to draw a load up—Distance from Fort Smith
to the South Fork of the Canadian river, 75 miles, on the
military road, which is very bad for travel.

Saturday, June 3d—made 6 miles and stopped over Sunday.
After passing over the south fork of the river, out of the
" Choctaw Nation," we then came into the Chicasaw, when
I bought an Indian pony for $30. Sunday 4th—business of
the day, washing, cooking, &c. Mr. Fenn, one of Mr. Os-
born's company killed a deer.

June 4th. Started at 6½ o'clock A. M. and drove across
two or three small prairies, passed through a low bottom, very
muddy, and crossed a small creek called Cold creek by Lieu-
tenant Dent—thence over a prairie in the afternoon, and another small stream when we stopped for the night, having accomplished eighteen miles. John Stewart here got frighten-
ed at the violent commotion of a tree near at hand, to a limb
of which the oxen had been tied. All hands were on the
move, expecting an opportunity for the shooting of a panther.
Mr. Stewart thought he saw one, and fired his rifle and only
on the startling of the animals at the report, discovered the
real cause of his apprehension.

Tuesday, June 5th. Started at 6 A. M.—traveled over a
prairie, through a bottom and crossed several ravines. In the
afternoon passed over a lofty mountain which had been in
view ever since we started. Our progress was arrested during the afternoon by a violent thunder storm, accompanied
by heavy rain—made nine miles and passed the night in the
woods.

June 6th. Sarted about 5½ o'clock in the morning, traveling over rocks, hill, swamps, and small creeks whose banks
in several instances were so steep that we were obliged to let
the teams down by ropes—went about two miles and stopped
at Shawnee village, in the Shawnee Nation. This comprises
only two houses and a few scatered huts in the woods. Traveled 12 miles and halted in the woods.

June 7th. Started early and continued our devious route over streams, rocks, rivers and prairie land, which latter was here strewn thickly over with prairie flowers—accomplished twelve miles, rested for the night, in order to recruit the mules which became sadly jaded by reason of hard driving.

June 8th. Off again.at 6½ o'clock A. M. crossed several small prairies, and a number of creeks. The banks of these were like the previous ones, excessively steep, the water muddy and the bed covered deep with slime, save in one instance which was clear and limped having a fine gravelly bottom, resembling those we have in the north.

The Shawnee Indians are dressed with leggings and that includes nearly all their covering save a shirt or sash for the lower portion of the waist. Distance accomplished, ten miles.

June 9th. Laid over to make a division in our company, and repair a wheel of our ox wagon. Mr. Osborn and myself were out eight or nine miles to examine the road and found it bad. Got a refreshing drenching in a thunder shower.

Sunday, 10th. Repaired our wheel. Thunder and rain throughout the day.

11th. Completed our division after a great deal of difficulty, and closed the concern by selling to the highest bidder.— Started at 3 o'clock in the afternoon with the ox train—drew Mr. Dutcher and Vandercar out of the mud, passed them, and stopped to repair a pole that he had broken, and to alter wagons into carts, traveled over a prairie and several muddy bottoms, and got a kick from one of the oxen which lamed me so that I could scarcely walk. Went on about five miles and stopped in a fine grass prairie over night.

June 12th. Resumed our journey at 5 A. M., with the ox train. Felt very lame in my knee which pained me exceedingly. Passing over Prairie and low land we arrived at the Delaware mountain, where we found a beautiful stream of clear, cold water, not inferior to any which can be found in New York State, crossed several others in the forenoon. The distance from Fort Smith to Delaware mountain is 139 miles, and from the mountain to Chatau 35, making an entire distance of 174 miles. In the afternoon we proceeded 12 miles, found the roads somewhat improved, encamped during the night on a prairie.

June 13th. Morning clear with a high wind. Traveled over a prarie and passed thence into a low bottom or oak shrubbery—broke the top of my wagon and halted in a prairie at noon to repair it. Resumed our journey—crossed an inconsiderable creek and put up for the night—advanced 16 miles.

June 14th. The morning cloudy, ominous clouds in the distance, threatening thunder and rain. We continued our rout from 7 A. M. until 1 P. M. and dined on a prarie—pushed on in the afternoon despite heavy rain and found the roads unusualy good for this section. Travelled 16 miles and encamped for the night in a prairie where we discovered a kind of claycy substance of a reddish color, much resembling the brick clay we have in the north. The land appears to have been washed as there are a great number of deep cuts all over the prairie lands in this nation.

June 15th. The weather somewhat hazy and cold,—grass very wet. We traveled during the morning on the same prairie over a good road. Fell in with an Indian bearing a deer which we purchased and halted for dinner. Pressed forward in the afternoon until we arrived at a branch of the Canadian river, where there was so high a freshet that we were obliged to lay over—traveled 15 miles. Mr. Stewart and myself went out a short time in search of deer. I saw three, shot at one and missed it. Mr. Stewart lost himself, and during the night was compelled to climb a tree to evade the attack of several wolves which surrounded him. Five men from different companies went in search of him, who discovered his retreat, but were no more successful than himself in striking the right course, having all to remain until morning before they could find their way back.

June 16th. Started a little before 4 o'clock in search of deer—saw one on the prairie, but were not fortunate enough to capture any—got wet through and returned to build a bridge across a branch of the Canadian River, this being the only way of crossing, there being from 10 to 15 feet of water. We worked hard all day—blistered our hands terribly, but had the satisfaction of seeing the bridge completed before nightfall—took supper and rested for the night moderately considering the attacks of mosquitoes.

June 17th. Sunday morning, started and drove two miles, in order to cross our bridge before the water carried it away, which having accomplished we halted for the Sunday. In company with three others, I started to ascertain where Chateau trading house was situated. We proceeded as far as the Canadian River, where we found the water so high that we were not able to ford the current. It is a considerable river, and the water is as red as brick.

18th. Monday, laid over to recruit our mules in a prairie in Camanche Nation, where we washed and repaired our wagons, and put our guns in order in case of an attack from the Indians.

June 19th. Laid over still to recruit and to ascertain where the route ran, likewise to fall in with more company if there should be any in the vicinity. Myself and another in our company went out in search of deer. Just as the sun was sinking, I came up with an old bear and cub. The bear I shot but not mortally. However I had quite an exciting time. After I had wounded her, she rose upon her hind feet and came towards me gnashing her teeth and growling furiously, the cub running up into a tree in terror. If I had not been so remiss in re-loading, ample time was afforded me for several fine shots before she made off, but it being now well nigh dark I was reluctantly compelled to leave her. It was not less in a direct line than two miles from the camp, and in consequence of a deep ravine between myself and it, I was obliged to describe a circle of some five or more. On arriving at the camp I found the folks in no little consternation, having begun to entertain fears that I was lost, and on the eve of dispatching messengers to seek me. It was then about 9 or 10 o'clock.

June 20th. Wednesday, started to cross the Canadian river at 8 A. M., traveled four miles, got our wagons and mules into the river and were obliged to unload our baggage and carry it ashore. The bottom of the river is formed of quicksand which renders it almost impossible for teams laden at all heavily to pass over.

June 21st. Laid over on account of Mr. Osborn's illness.— Two others, together with myself, rode out about 16 miles to ascertain if there were any other companies on the old road, but returned without discovering any.

June 22d. Laid over Mr. Osborn still continuing ill. Settled with Mr. Stewart for the oxen and in full for all accounts, and with all others of our party up to this time.

June 23d. Still continuing at Chateau in the hope that Mr. Osborn who is becoming better will be well enough in a day or two to admit of our continuing our journey.

We have been considerably annoyed to-day by upwards of 100 of different tribes of Indian Squaws and Papooses belong-to the Washington, Quampau and Kickapas, who are on their return home from hunting. The spectacle is somewhat disgusting to one who has lived in a civilized country, being mostly in a state of nudity, both men and women, the only covering consisting of a blanket or band of colored cloth, partially enveloping the nether portion of the body and fastened at the waste with a strap. Children from 14 and downward are entirely destitute of garments—the only appendage being a string of beads, a bunch of feathers or some ornament encircling the neck or arms or pending from the ears. They are the most intolerable nuisance to which we have hitherto been subjected. They pester the whole camp with unceasing and clamerous demands for tobacco or food, and they will not be refused. They are the most improtunate set of beggars that ever urged entreaty. We have to keep a sharp eye upon all their movements, constantly, to prevent their purloining anything and everything portable.

June 24th. Sunday, the Indians still remain with us, and if they are not a filthy set then I never saw any. So thronged are they with vermin that the motion of walking dislodges them in multitudes, on which occasion the preying not unfrequently become a prey. Al 4½ o'clock we started and placed six good miles between us and their camp.

June 25th. Resumed our travel at 5½ o'clock in the morning and drove straight on over a prairie until noon when we halted, but found no water that was palatable. We pushed on until night, making 21 miles when we stopped till morning without either wood or water in the vicinity of the camp. We have been traveling for two days in the general hunting Ground for both Indians and Whites. Far as the eye can penetrate, is an outspread plain, seemingly without limit or boundary·

June 26th. Started at 4 A. M. moving onward over the same prairie which we have been traversing for days past. At 10 o'clock we came to a small ravine where we found a stream of water—cooked dinner, and filled our water sacks for cooking the evening supper. In the afternoon, through a heavy thunder shower, proceeded 16 miles and encamped on the prairie for the night, without wood or water.

June. 27th. The weather wet and cloudy—started at 6 o'clock and found the prairie very wet and muddy, until afternoon when we struck a rolling prairie—found a fine road—and after accomplishing a distance of 18 miles rested for the night.

June 28th. Continued our route at $4\frac{1}{2}$ A. M. this day, and after driving about three hours , found a very wet and muddy road which lead us across the Canadian river, on the south side, where, after leaving the bottom, which is mostly covered with water, we found a good road on prairie land, and by night had made 18 miles, where we stopped near some mounds or pyramids that somewhat resemble a light house off Sandy Hook, being composed of red rock. They have probably been thrown up by some volcanic eruption and vary from 75 to 150 feet in height.

June 29th. Started at 5 o'clock on a good prairie road and saw a herd of some animals which resembled deer, save in color, which at the distance we were removed, appeared nearly white. We concluded from Fremont's description that they must have been either Elks or Antelopes. In the afternoon we saw a great number of the latter, but could not get a shot at one of them. Drove 18 miles, and stopped over night, unprovided with either wood or water, save a small quantity that we had in our wagon and a little water that we dipped from a mud hole.

June 30th. Moved off at $4\frac{1}{2}$ A. M., drove 10 miles and neared a small creek, where we remained until Monday morning. Here we saw a number of Antelopes and discovered signs of Buffaloes. The water is hard in consequence of its being impregnated with lime stone of which the bed of the stream mainly consists.

July 1st. Nothing worthy of notice—made spokes for one wheel and rested for the remainder of the day.

July 2d, Started at 4 o'clock and crossed three branches of the Red river, which are all within three miles of each other The banks are all very steep and high, varying from 20 to 50 feet, so that it is impossible for trains to get up over them. We proceeded to Red river, distance about two miles from the camp, which is a stream of considerable magnitude. We passed on over a prairie, destitute of food for cattle, or water, and halted till morning, having driven 18 miles.

July 3d. Continued our route at $4\frac{1}{2}$ A. M. over a dry prairie, and saw an antelope and a wolf. In crosing a ravine my

wagon was upset, and its load turned upside down, without
injuring the vehicle and but slightly wetting the contents. In
consequence of a very severe thunder storm we were compelled to remain here until the next day. The thunder is most
appalling and the lightning terrific in the extreme. It seemed as though the very plain tottered beneath us, and the
heavens were lit up by one blinding and perpetual blaze of
livid light. This is a fearful place for this elemental confla-
gation. Not a day, I believe has passed us on the prairies,
without a thunder storm.

Wednesday, July 4th. Started at 5 o'clock, road good—
drove about two miles and arrived at a branch of Red river,
where we were obliged to wait until the water fell before we
considered it safe or practicable to ford, the river being from
10 to 15 feet in depth. At half past five in the afternoon we
forded, it having fallen about 3 feet. The bottom being of quick
sand it required four yoke of oxen and one of the mules to
draw the wagon. We drove twelve miles by which time it
near midnight, and finding a suitable place for camping,
abounding with wood and water—halted during the night
which we passed pretty comfortably, saving that we were annoyed at intervals by a panther that prowled around the
camp.

July 5th. Continued our journey over a fine rolling prairie,
interspersed by mounds , several feet in height, composed of
stone resembling Paris plaster or lime. The prairie is a barren tract of land which might not inappropriately be called a
desert, since it commonly affords but scanty nourishment, and
a still scantier supply of water. I had like to forgot to mention that one of our party killed a very large wolf—wounding
him three times. He measured three feet in height. We
started at three in the afternoon, and drove until 7 in the
evening, when we arrived at a beautiful bottom, where we
found luxuriant grass in abundance for the cattle. The bottom is about one mile in width, and running through it is a
considerable stream which we called Dry Rriver. Traveled
20 miles.

July 6th. Resumed our route at $3\frac{3}{4}$ in the morning and
passed pleasantly through a somewhat picturesque prairie—
the scene here was very beautiful, skirting the river, while
flowers and wild p`ums were abundant. Our route now lay
over a very high prairie, on which rose up to a commanding
height some high mountains of stone that resemble those we

have down East. Here, congregated in great numbers, we found Buzzards, birds of grotesque appearnce, snakes and other reptiles. We traveled until eleven o'clock when we stopped beside a mud puddle, without any wood for fires. In the afternoon we had proceeded but a short distance when the thunder and lightning re-commenced. We made 13 miles however, and stopped on the prairie without wood or water.

July 7th. Started at 4½ A. M. and had driven but a short distance, when Robt. VanderCook said he saw a bear ahead. Robt. and myself went out to reconnoitre, and seeing nothing of him, were about to give up, when we alighted upon the track of an animal which proved to be a buffalo. We held on over a very hilly and rolling prairie until about 9 o'clock, when we came up with the other ox teams ahead, and halted to take in a supply of food and water for the animals, while we crossed a desert of sand, some distance before us, about twen-miles in length. We here found an abundant supply of wild plums, that are most delicious, when ripe, but for which we were about a week too early. The cactus, heliotrope and most other flowers that we cultivate in the East, grow here spontaneously. We passed a number of prairie dog villages, their holes or habitations being laid out with all the regularity of streets. They are a diminutive little animal, about the size of a woodchuck, and of a reddish color.

After driving 24 miles we came to a ravine which, much to our surprise, supplied us with food and water for our animals, and where we halted for the night.

Sunday, July 8th. This day we resolved to continue here as the good pasture would tend to recruit the strength of the cattle, which had much impaired by reason of hard driving and indifferent forage. We this day killed a dear which furnished us with a supply of fresh food for the camp.

July 9th. Started at half-past three in the morning and crossed two branches of Dry river, the beds of each consisting of quick sand, which was very hard work to drive through, and fell in with an orchard of wild plums of delicious flavor. We drove on until 10 oclock, when we halted, but without wood or water.

Resuming our rout in the afternoon we passed on over a hard, sandy road, through a barren prairie, with the exception of an occasional plum orchard. We have been traveling for several days over a mountain range which attains to a considerable altitude. When viewed from a distance, they present the appearance of fortifications or battlemented towers.— They are principally composed of lime, sand and a substance to which Fremont gives the name of pudding stone. Somewhere in this vicinity, we discovered a tree on the bark of which some company that preceded us had written, or cut out that they found stuck on a pole a few days previous a human scalp, recently affixed there by the Indians,which, accorto their custom, denoted open hostilities with the whites.

The following day we proceeded until about noon over a sandy bottom near the Canadian river, where we again halted.. On a tree we found an account of a fracas between a Texian company numbering about sixty, and a band of Kioways and Mexicans about half that number, in which the latter sustained a signal repulse.

Leaving the high table land or rocky wall on the right of the river, our route again lay over a low bottom. After proceeding about 22 miles the intense heat rendered traveling extremely laborious, so finding it impracticable to proceed farther, we encamped for the night.

The day following we proceeded at an early hour. A refreshing breeze having sprung up during the night, the odor of the full scented prairie flowers was borne gratefully on the gale. About noon we suspended our journey in order to water the cattle, and refresh ourselves from a clear, cold spring than which we have met with none better, even in the Empire State. Some of our company who were a little in advance saw three bears and a deer, and were able to come within gun shot of the latter but failed in killing it.

July 12th. Started about 5 o'clock, having first broken fast on some good pancakes and a cup of excellent coffee. The route this day lies through a low land furnishing neither water nor pasturage fit for use, and crossed by a heavy miry road. Through the bottom runs the Canadian river, which here attains a width of about forty or fifty rods. The bed of the stream has a thick incrustation of salt. On either side of us extends a range of mountains which imparts an aspect of dreariness and barrenness to this desolate tract of country. In the afternoon we harnessed up, and after driving little more than a mile, arrived at the foot of the mountain. Here we experienced another terrific storm of thunder and lightning, accompanied by tremendous rain and tempestuous wind. In

consequence of the severity of the storm we were compelled to suspend traveling, and retired to rest, as well as we
could, for the night, completely drenched and jaded.

The next day we pushed onward up the mountain, which
required a double team to ascend—arrived at the summit, we
entered upon an extensive rolling prairie—accomplished a
distance of 24 miles through a dense mist, without meeting
with water or forage. We saw one wild sheep, but could not
get near enough to it to render a shot effective.

July 14th. A strong wind from the eastward, accompanied,
however, by heavy mist; at 9 A. M., reached a small inlet,
called by the Hivilah company Crane creek, where we found
wood and excellent water in abundance. Here we remained
until afternoon, and cooked dinner—continuing our route until 4 P. M., we arrived at a good camping ground, where we
found excellent pasturage, wood, water, and orchards laden
with both wild plum and cherry. We met also with a great
number of various kinds of cactus, which in hue and exuber-
ance of growth surpassed anything I ever saw before of this
description of flower.

On the following morning we cooked our beans, dried apples,
&c. During the day we saw several troops of prairie dogs,
and a great number of Dahlias and Cactuses, many of the
latter exceding six feet in height. After advancing about
12 miles we encamped near a small ravine.

The next day presented much the same series of events, saving that we saw severel fine deer and antelopes in different
herds. At 10 A. M. we halted for refreshment. The Cactus
served us for fuel, being the only combustible material we
could obtain. While resting we were surprised suddenly by
an ox that rushed towards our encampment, but being alarmed
at our confusion took himself off at full speed. He was pursued swiftly by four of our company on horseback, captured
and brought back to the camp. Probably it had strayed
away from some band of California Emigrants in the spring.
After remaining here all night, we set off the following day,
but fell in with nothing worthy of note. Met with one or two
buffaloes and several goats. After making about twenty
miles, a sudden thunder shower caused us to encamp till the
following morning. Advanced about twenty miles, and at
night killed the captured ox and dressed it.

This morning, July 19th. Mr. Osborn came up with us,

not having seen him since we parted at Chateau. I killed a rattle snake this morning. Found ourselves at night about 22 miles in advance.

The rout on the ensuing day was through an unfertile tract of low country, bounded on the left by a lofty ridge terminating in a high table land. We halted at noon, and by the aid of such fuel as the cactus would admit, washed, cooked and made some excellent soup from the ox shank, which, together with a cup of good coffee, furnished us a first rate dinner. Rested at 6 P. M. for the night.

July 21st. Started this morning at 4 o'clock over a picturesque prairie, in a clear bright sunshine, and a bracing breeze. To-day's travel has afforded more magnificent scenery than any we have yet seen. Extending far away to the left is a mountain range terminating in lofty table land, its base garnished with healthful looking shrubbery and its sides adorned by majestic Cedar. The mountains from their appearance would favor the belief that they are occasionally the theatre of volcanic eruptions. Passing over a small creek, the water of which is of a reddish tinge—we pushed on over the table land, and having made 15 miles, pitched our camp for the night.

In consequence of heavy rain which continued throughout the next day, we laid over, and prepared a soup dinner, which we discussed with no slight relish.

July 23d, and 24th. Accomplished about 40 miles, through scenery slightly varied, and on the latter day killed a very large ratlesnake.

On the 25th we proceeded about 25 miles further over a high prairie, abounding in cactus, cedar and pine. These supplied us with fuel and water which we were fortunate enough to discover in a puddle, and was eagerly appropriated to culinary purposes.

July 26th. We arrived this noon at a large creek, where we dicovered sheep tracks, and some one's foot prints. This is the first indication or trace of civilization with which we have been cheered since we left Chateau, distant from this about six hundred miles. Despite a sudden storm of rain we pushed on vigorously, and towards sundown, as we arrived on the brow of a hill, we saw before us a Mexican herdsman driving a herd of more than two hundred cattle. As he could not speak the English tongue, and we understood nothing of Spanish, we could procure but little information touching the distance to Santa Fe. He camped beside a large rock , some skins serving him for his bedding, and possessed of a few cooking utensils.

On the following day, after traveling a short distance, we came in sight of great numbers of sheep, in droves of several hundreds, under the charge of drivers. Soon afterwards we overhauled a Mexican who was driving his sheep to Santa Fe. Luckily he spoke English, and we ascertained from him that we could not reach that place in less than three days, in consequence of the road being exceedingly stony—the way principally being over the Gaudalope mountains.

A little in advance of the driver we had an opportunity afforded us of seeing a Mexican Lady. She was somewhat pretty, and was mounted on a horse, beside her husband. After halting for refreshment, we moved on in the afternoon, and drove over the mountain, when we came on a Mexican Settlement. They were anxious to sell us American whiskey, for which they charge two dollars a glass. They live in miserable mud huts, about 12 feet in height. They have a church constructed of the same material, of similar stunted dimensions, surmounted by a cross, but destitute of windows or even openings for the admission of light, there being but one small aperture for this purpose. The road just at this spot is good and continues so hence to the Puerco river, on the right bank of which stands the little town of San Miguel. The prospect of the surrounding country to-day is most delightful — Undulating fields of corn and wheat glisten beautifully in the sunlight and the trees are of a loftier altitude and larger growth than those we have seen hitherto. After traveling twenty two miles we rested till morning, or rather noon next day. In the meanwhile some of us have paid a visit to San Miguel, a thriving village situate on the right bank of the Purco river, flowing through the Guadalope mountains in New Mexico. The houses are constructed of an adhesive description of mud which is wrought to a certain consistence, cut into layers about one foot square and three inches in thickness. These are dried in a kiln and then piled up in quadrangular blocks for building walls for dwelling houses. Small poles reach horizontally from either side of the building to serve as a foun dation for the roof, which consists likewise of mud tiles. The houses seldom exceed one story, or from 10 to 14 feet in height.

There are quite a number of Stores in this place who retail goods furnished from St. Louis or Santa Fe, at most exorbitant rate. As a sample of their charges I remarked that Soap was six shillings a bar—Bacon, twenty cents per lb.— Eggs three for a shilling.

The village is so laid out as to form an unbroken barrier of buildings around the outskirts, so as to prevent the hostile incursions of the Indians, of whom they live in considerable apprehension. They have a church supplied with a bell which is rung every evening. The edifice is built in the Gothic style, surmounted by a cross and furnished with a spacious yard for the use of interment.

They have a tavern which the landlord showed me, that would be somewhat of a curiosity in a civilized country. The bar room is about twelve feet square, the bar occupying one corner, where whiskey (the only liquor it furnishes,) may be obtained for one shilling a glass. Beyond this is a room about 12 feet by 30, set apart for fandangos &c. This room can boast of a coat of whitewash, a piece of extravagance seldom countenanced in this quarter. Connected with the Tavern is a large yard for the accommodation of the mules &c. of the guests.

Some attention is paid to farming, and the cultivation of land. Their principal crops, corn and wheat, are very fine. They have goats and cattle in great abundance, the former they are obliged to watch narrowly, as the Indians not unfrequently carry off from one to two hundred of them at a time.

After returning from San Miguel, a large train of Santa Fe traders, from St. Louis, about thirty five in number, loaded with various descriptions of merchandise, with teams bearing six or seven thousand pounds weight, drawn by three or more yoke of oxen, came up to our camp. They left St. Louis on the 22d of May being the same as that in which we left Fort Smith. We resumed our route in the afternoon and crossed the river, leaving Mr. Osborn to follow on the next Monday. We passed several Mexican houses before nightfall, when we halted.

July 29th. We started at 7 A. M., and halted after driving about ten miles, near the ruins of Porcos, an old palace sacked by the Indians upwards of a hundred years ago. The building extends about half a mile in length and a quarter of a mile in breadth. The fire is said to have been fed unintermittingly, until the entire edifice was utterly consumed. In passing it we picked up several of the flint arrow heads used by the Indians in warfare.

LeavingPorcos the next day, we passed onward and neared the pass, where Armigo intended to give battle to Gen. Kirney, but who fled without leading on to an assault. We remained here for the night, but were annoyed by the long howl of the wolves, that probably were attracted by the carcasses of several oxen, scattered around, probably left by some party of Californians.

July 31st. Started early, and passing on through the mountains, crossed a mound wherein are interred two unfortunate California emigrants. The mountains are covered with large timber and abundance of grass may be discovered in the defiles, but water is very scarce. After journeying fifteen miles we encamped for the night at Santa Fe.

The military display, when we first came in sight of the city, wore something of an American aspect, there being about six hundred soldiers. We drove into the city along the borders of a small stream and stopped for the night.

On the following morning we traversed the city in the hope of getting some corn for our animals, but found none save in one place, at a charge of $6 the *fanaka*, or four shillings the *almo*. The houses are all built of mud, having no glass windows, but a number of round perpendicular glass pillars in lieu of them. The inhabitants comprise the lowest and vilest characters, whose time is mainly occupied in gambling, drunken fandangoes and debaucheries.

In the afternoon we started for Galisteo, and finding after going upwards of seven miles that we were on the wrong road, stopped for the night without either food water or fuel.

Started the next morning to discover the right road and suffered extreme fatigue in consequence of the heat and our long fast, but after travelling about eight miles we found water and fuel upon which we halted for the night, and pursued our journey at 2 P. M. the day following—our search for the right road was still unsuccessful and after beating about for six or eight miles, we returned to last night's encampment.

Early in the morning, Robert and I started in search of the road or of some one who could give us some information respecting it. We travelled as far as Santa Fe, where we found a number of Californians that came in company with us, who were going to return to the States. We hired a room and concluded to return to Santa Fe to try to dispose of our articles. We returned to camp and all were satisfied with our arrangement.

The following morning we returned to Santa Fe; arrived there about noon and made arrangements for the night. We disposed of our oxen and wagon to a party of Californians who had given up the expedition.

August 7th. To-day we commenced overhauling our wearing apparel, tools, &c. By the 10th we had got matters so arranged that we were determined to make an attempt to get out of Santa Fe, where we could procure provender for our animals at less expense. We now commenced packing our animals for the first time, and had some difficulty with two of our mules that were very wild, having only purchased them the day before for $100. We succeeded at length in effecting our preparations, and, taking the Albiquique Road, made fifteen miles that day.

The next morning, after another scene with the mules, we started for Galisteo, but had not proceeded far when one of them took fright and running off with his pack, spilt more than half our coffee before we could succeed in catching him. After travelling twenty-one miles we found ourselves at Galisteo, where we stopped to recruit the animals and wait for Mr. Stewart. Here we fell in with two companies, the Hevilah company, from New York, and the Morgan County Rangers, numbering in all seventeen wagons, with which they purposed proceeding as far on as possible.

August 13th. Occupied in fresh padding our pack saddles.

August 14th. Laboring under a severe cold, in consequence of a thorough wetting from last night's rain. We are busy at work with some canvass for a tent, but not having sufficient of this material, I have given for that purpose the sheets presented to me by my sister Emiline, having no use for them here, beds being unfashionable on the Plains. This morning Mr. Stewart arrived at the camp. About evening we received information from one of a company from Fort Smith, that Mr. Nutting, a gentleman with whom I was acquainted, was in the vicinity of our camp, and moreover that they had met Messrs. Kendall, Scoughton, and Stewart, about fifty miles from Santa Fe, and that they had lost one of their men, named Dutcher, and buried him near San Miguel.

On the 15th we completed our tent and took shelter beneath it for the night. Though small it afforded us comfortable lodging. The next day we remained in camp. Robert Blake went to Santa Fe to sell articles and purchase others for the journey. On the afternoon of the day following Mr. Nutting came to our camp with letters from brother Charles, Mrs. Woodward, Mr. Hart, and one other. All were received with much pleasure.

We still remain here waiting for our animals to recruit themselves, who are sorely jaded with travel, and also for more company, with whom to continue our route. R. Blake has returned without disposing of his goods but has obtained all that he required.

August 19th. Suffer much from rheumatism in my shoulders, arms and back. We remained here until the 30th of August, and then collecting our stock of valuables, started for Alberquique, about 2 P. M., drove eight miles and pitched our tent at night in a beautiful mountain gorge.

The next day we made twenty-one miles, and on the one following, while waiting for Mr. Stewart, had excellent sport in shooting wild fowl, killing five Curlews and seven Brants, which supplied us with two glorious pot-pies. On this and the following day we made forty-six miles and halted on the night of the second of September close by the ruins of Pueblo. We saw several deer during the day but did not kill any.

Sept. 3d. We crossed over a range of mountains covered with cedar and pine shrubs into a defile, watered by a small stream. Halting here over night, we resumed our journey early in the morning and passed the mountain about 11 A. M. The next day, just here, we had the good fortune to kill a fine Antelope which we carried onward to our noon encampment and made an excellent dinner on the pluck, heart, &c. After proceeding some thirty-three miles, we arrived at the bank of the Rio Del Norte about 9 P. M.

Sept. 5th. After travelling six or seven miles we fell in with good water and pasturage for the animals, and where we stopped to feed and jerk some of our Antelope, that it might be more portable.

To-day being the 22d, commemorate of Robert's birth day, we regaled ourselves with a cup of good coffee and a loin steak of venison. After making sixteen miles, we crossed the Rio

Del Norte, over which, together with our baggage, we were conveyed in a small ferry boat. The animals had to swim across, and landed safe on the opposite bank. We camped about two miles from the spot, falling in with Doctor Pope's wagon train from North Carolina.

The day following we drove along the river side and stopped at noon in a small grove of cotton wood. We passed several villages, where we purchased onions at five cents for two, and some delicious grapes. We proceeded in the afternoon until within one mile of Secora, where we came up with a wagon train and camp, waiting for other pack mule companies.

Sept. 7th, 8th and 9th. Remained here encamped anxiously awaiting a company which we expected to travel with.— Peaches are scarce here and indifferent, but grapes are plentiful. Mr. Stewart, his son, and three others of the company, have got sick of pack mules and bought a wagon to travel in company with a wagon train. The country here is mountainous, the river running through a low valley covered with cotton wood. To-day we had the pleasure of seeing the notorious Armizo, and the Governor of New Mexico, who passed in a carriage on their way to church.

On the afternoon of the 10th we started and passed through the town of Secora. While passing, an American, discharged soldier, fired a gun at some Mexicans, the ball striking very near our party. There is an election held here to-day, for the purpose of sending Delegates to the United States, for the formation of a territorial government. To-day we accomplished only eight miles, and halted on the river bottom, where we purchased a *fanagar* of Mexican flour for $6.

Sept. 11th. After a good night's rest on the soft grass on the banks of the Rio Del Norte, and partaking of coffee and a mess of fine "dodgers," we pushed on until we arrived at the town of San Antonio, where some of our company obtained flour at a Mexican mill, which would be considered rather a "small affair" in the States. During the day we had a heavy fall of rain, which rendered the road so slippery that we halted for the night.

The next morning we were awoke by the violent pelting of the rain, whereupon we crawled out in rather better season than usual. It prevented us from going on until afternoon, when we advanced about twelve miles, and on the following day made about fifteen more.

Sept. 14th. We met to-day with rather an unpleasant cir-
cumstance. Two of our mules had been stolen during the
night. We found their trail about 9 o'clock, but on returning to the camp we found that two others had been made away
with ; so about twelve of us, well armed, went off in pursuit.
After proceeding twenty-five miles, reaching the highest of the
mountain, and hearing the Indians in the brush below us,
we stopped for consultation as to whether we should proceed
upon them or return. At this moment, on seeing us, they left
the mules and fled, leaving them badly injured.

During the two following days we made about forty miles
and on the afternoon of the second came up with a tributary
stream of the Rio Grande. The 18th of September is our last
and fourteenth day along this river.

On the morning of the 19th we made in a Southerly direction over high sand hills, the sun being very fierce and op-
pressive. Coming to a rock, in a large cavity of which we
found a beautiful supply of rain water, we halted until afternoon, and encamped after proceeding twelve miles.

On the following day we travelled about fifteen miles and
encamped, having some apprehensions of the Indians.

On the 21st we made twenty-one miles and arrived at the
Rio Membras river, beating the wagon train by four hours.—
During the remainder of the day, throughout the night, and
the day following we had incessant rain.

Sunday, Sept. 22d. To-day our guide leaves us. We are
encompassed by the Ohavaca Mountains. We cut two fine
sticks for tent poles, which we have had to carry about three-
fourths of a mile.

Sept. 24th. Proceeded fifteen miles over a prairie, hemmed
in on either side by a range of lofty mountains. when we
reached an eminence which is called Ben More Peak. We
halted, but without either wood or water. In the afternoon
passed the grave of a Californian by the name of Handley,
and travelled until dark, in the hope of finding water, but
without success, and halted for the night, having travelled
twenty-seven miles without finding any.

The following morning, after proceeding six miles, we fell
in with water, which we dipped out of a mud puddle and
watered the animals. We now cooked breakfast, and got a
pot-pie from three partridges, which I had killed the day before, and some coffee. In the afternoon we reached a

stream of water, where the wagon train concluded to halt and take into consideration Mr. VanderCar's case, who had loaded his team so heavily as to break them down and prevent him from keeping up with the party.

Sept. 26th. This morning we are still in camp, not having been able to arrange concerning Van's team. The weather is cold and rainy. We have been obliged to buy another mule, in consequence of one of the ponies giving out. We paid $55 for it.

Sept. 27th, 28th and 29th. Weather continues very rainy; made about forty miles, and crossed and re-crossed a small creek six or seven times during the route.

Sunday, Sept. 30th. The weather clear and cold—we started at 6¾ in the morning, and while passing over a heavy road saw at a distance either a herd of wild cattle or Indians, probably the latter.

The streams we passed yesterday are the first that we have crossed running into the Gila. Arriving at the foot of a mountain, the base of which is laved by a fine stream, we halted, and after noon resumed our journey. The road here takes a westerly course. Crossing the mountain we arrived at Gaudaloupe Passs, accomplishing twenty miles.

Monday, Oct. 1st. The country still continues mountainous and the road is the most rugged that we have yet met with and all pretty much down hill. Timber is somewhat scarce, and principally consists of cedar shrubberies and a dwarfish species of oak. Cactus fruit is abundant. Moving onward we descended a low ravine, skirted by sycamores and watered by a small stream; the grass, however, being indifferent. Here we halted to noon. In the afternoon we drove along the margin of the stream which is here bordered by a lofty mountain on either side, and massive rocks piled one above another to an immense height. In the course of the day we crossed this stream fifty-two times.

Oct. 2d. This morning after crossing the creek some seventeen times we ascended a high bluff and left it behind us.— Proceeding over a barren plain we struck a ravine, furnishing broad grass and water. After a halt we moved on until we came in sight of the ruins of San Barnido, which was deserted on account of the incessant attacks of Indians. It has the appearance of being a large town originally. A flat bottom beneath the ruins bears traces of having been once under good cultivation. Saw a large bear prowling through the ruins; went on to the mountain and camped till morning.

Oct. 3. Traveled until late in the evening when we arrived at Black Water creek, a distance of 22 miles.

Oct. 4th. This morning we remained in camp until late, owing to several of our company having gone in pursuit of wild cattle which they had heard during the night. They saw several and wounded one pretty severely, but returned without killing any. On arriving at the second crossing of the Black Water Creek, we halted till afternoon, when we again moved forward, but had proceeded only a short distance when we discovered a w.ld b.ll. Mr. Jones, fired but missed the animal, some four or five gave chase for five or six miles. Colonel Bonner fired five shots wou.ding him in the shoulder, and in the excitement, sent a bullet through the neck of his mule, but it inflicted no ser.ous injury. The Bull dashed into a thicket of thorn bushes and we were obliged to discontinue the pursuit. We joined the teams towards evening, at the encampment.

The following day we made 20 miles, and camped for the night near a pool of water, and watered the mules, there being no more water for upwards of twenty miles ahead.

Oct. 5th. We drove on until we arrived at the San Pedro river, where we halted to repair wagons and rest our mules, one of them had stumbled during the day, from excessive fatigue. The road, here runs north of the village of Tueson, and the river empties into the Gila.

Sunday the 7 h. We remained in camp, the weather warm and rainy—with little to occupy our thoughts of a pleasant nature, save reminiscences of good old times, and the memories of home. Towards noon to-day, the Havilah Company and Mr. Osborn came up with us. Their guide had misled them on a trail, ran away with a horse and about $40 worth of property. Their mules were jaded, foot sore, and six of them had given out on the road. The company were short of provisions, and had not eaten anything for thirty hours, or until this noon.

The following day we started at an early hour, and traveled over a muddy road until noon, when we came up with part of the Illinois and the Missouri company, with oxen, from whom we ascertained that we were off from Cook's route, and on the road to Santa Cruz.

Oct. 9th. Started at 7 o'clock. Two of our men were out hunting yesterday, and have not returned. After traveling until noon, came up with Governor Edwards from Missouri, and encamped; when our hunters came up to us with the intelligence that they had killed a wild bull, about six miles from the camp, and taking mules they went back after the meat. We moved on in the afternoon, until within 2 miles of Santa Cruz, and camped. R. Blake and myself going into the town for provisions.

Oct. 10. We remained over until noon, in order to provide food for the camp. Blake and myself brought flour, (musty) Beans, Peas and Quinces. Started in the afternoon passed through the town and followed the Santa Cruz river about 10 miles—Camped.

Oct. 11. Weather fine and mild—continued our rout along the river, and pased a number of deserted ranches. In fact the whole valley was formerly occupied, but in consequence of the hostilities and incursions of the Indians, had been deserted. Santa Cruz is in constant fear of the Indians, (Appaches) by whom it was entered a few days since and despoiled of most of its mules and cattle.

The soil in the valley of the river, is exceedingly rich, the best I have seen in Mexico. The timber is sparce and scattering. On the river's banks are cotton and musketi trees. The latter furnishes a bean which resembles in appearance and flavor those we have in the north. We encamped in a grove of cotton wood at noon, and thence passed on over a good road, neared the grave of Mis. Mudget, who was one of a train which passed here some few days since. The grave had been completely turn open by the wolves. At sunset we halted for the night, with excellent wood & water at hand.

Oct. 12th. This morning we overtook a company of 11 wagons with oxen, from Ohio, and adjoining states, with their families, who reminded me of home. All the women looked healthy, one especially, who was well looking and scented off in style. Two little children, who formed part of the company; I could scarcely refrain from fondling, they being the first whites we had seen since we left the states. Came to a clump of cotton wood trees, and camped. Twenty miles.

Oct. 13. The morning clear and cold—the first frost we have seen for the season—the middle part of the day, however, is warm. We passed two deserted villages, some fine peach trees, and melon vines, and a new species of cactus measuring from two to fifteen feet in height, and from one to two in diameter, traversed by grooves in a spiral direcion from the top to the bottom.

On the day following we met with a little larger species of cactus, many of them attaining a height of thirty feet, and a diameter of from two to three, furnished in many instances with branches numbering, from eight to ten. Towards evening we encamped about a mile from an Indian village. The Indians soon found their way to camp and offered for sale Corn, Beans, Flour and Beef. They have a considerable drove of cattle. They are a mixture of Mexican, Pimo, Apache, &c., some clothed with pants and others having only a short garment. Some of our company attended at a war dance they had last evening over some Apache Indians they had taken prisoners. I could hear their constant " powwow " all the evening. One of the Indians showed some of our men quite a quantity of gold that a Spaniard had collected in the dry diggings at California. Twenty-one miles to-day.

Oct. 16. We have concluded to stay here until Wednesday, (there being no grass until we get to Pimo village, distant sixty one miles) and recrui tour mules. Indians are coming into our camp every few minutes. We have fallen in with a company from Illinois, from whom we learn that a small party had been cut off by the Apaches, (20 in number) on the Gila.

16th. We still remain in this place, a number of our mules having failed and one died.

On the 17th. We drove through the Indian village, and visited a convent, containing fifty five large images, with several smaller ones, numerous paintings, and a number of human sculls. The building must have been constructed by a good workman, inasmuch as it had stood fifty years, and is still in good order.

We slaughtered to-day 2 three year old beeves for which we paid $14.

Driving over a barren plain some five miles in extent, we encamped for the night by the side of a running stream, about one mile from the town of Tueson. Here the Mexicans came to our camp to trade with cotton goods at 3s. per yard; and other articles after a proportionate rate. They had flour, corn and some fine quinces, a few of which we purchased.

Oct. 18. Passing though the town of Tueson, we purchased some needful articles, and moved on over a heavy, sandy road, when Sqr. More's wagon became broken in the axel-tree. We had started from the 17th with a wagon, that Mr. Jones of North Carolina, had provided us.

Oct. 19. Stayed in camp to-day, as More had not finished his wagon, and our mules being in good grass, a luxury they would be compelled to forego for 33 miles to come.

20th. Traveled 22 miles.

21st. Pushed on in order to procure water, and after driving till ten o'clock without breakfast—found some, but it was al most impossible to use it, it being covered with a thick green scum. We were obliged to get dinner, and were compelled to use it as it was. On this and the day following, we traveled 47 miles, and found ourselves about 4 miles from the river Gila.

Oct. 23. We started about 8 A. M., and came into the Pimo village. The Indians here collected in great numbers, and came out to meet us. They led us into their village, and we took up our encampment with them for two days. Grass being unobtainable, we fed the animals on corn stalks which we purchased of the Indians. They came into our camp with green corn, pumpkins, melons, Kiln-drien wheat, peas, beans, dried corn, &c., sold in baskets or bags at such prices as you could bargan for. Corn, about three dollars a bushel, melons, from one to two shillings each; we traded sheets, vests, pants, coats and other articles, by way of banter, as money is well nigh useless to them.

They live in Lodges covered with weeds or straw, about 8 or 10 feet in height, of a conical shape. Their clothing is but scanty, some glorying in a blanket and vest or pantaloons, others in a shcet or coat. They seemed much pleased only to be able to sport a partial dress. They are of good size, tall and erect, with long black hair, descending almost to the knees. You have, however, to keep a sharp look out upon their movements, and your utmost vigilance will probably be insufficient to prevent their depredations. They will steal anything they can lay their hands on. Our company having lost blanket, axes and cooking utensils; complained to the chief, who made a long speech to some 3 or 4 hundred, charging them to restore the plundered property, but failing to persuade them to this act, he replaced the missing blankets by two of his own.

When I first got into the camp, I traded a mule with an Indian, for a pony,—the mule was poor and fagged out,—the next day he came with the mule and wanted to trade back,— this I refused to do. He then brought the chief who said if I would give him a shirt, he would be satisfied, I offered it to him and he refused. He then went to untie the pony, so I took out my revolvers and made him understand that if he did not leave it alone, I should give him six bullets for his pains. He then left, and again came back accompanied by the Chief, who told me that he would rather I should take both mule and pony, than the life of one of his people. I then offered him an extra sheet, which he accepted and left.

Oct. 25th. We started about 4 P. M. and drove out through the Pimo village, about 15 miles,—the next day the Maricopas came into the camp with corn, &c. for sale. We expect to remain here a day or two, as there is no water for the next 47, and no grass for the next 300 miles.

Oct. 27. Started this evening at 5 o'clock, and crossed 15 miles of the Journather, a barren desert, extending 41 miles. On the following day, traveled through the same barren prairie, through several mountain passes, and saw a good wagon, chains, yokes, &c. that had been abandoned by the way— stopped on the cannon at noon, and met with an Indian who told us it was 15 miles to water. About ten o'cock we made the river's bank, when we encamped after traveling 28 miles.

Oct. 29th. Started without breakfast over a sandy road, (chains, yokes and wagons, thrown away,) until eight—camped in the woods, at noon—went on after dinner, about eight miles, and halted at night, on the river's bank near the burial place of a Mr. Allen, of New York.

Oct. 30th. Started at 8 o'clock over a barren country— trunks, chests, shovels, picks and all kind of tools, lay by the road side, that had been abandoned. At noon we had a small Gila trout for dinner, which was remarkably good— went on about eight miles and camped near the burial places of Hickery and Davis,—the former stabbed Davis, who was tried by the Californians, pronunced guilty of murder, and was sentenced to be shot.

This was executed by drawing from the party two men who loaded six rifles wi h ball, and six with blank cartridges, the murderer was placed at a distance of twenty paces, and the shot entering the region of the heart, he expired immediately. They were both fr⌐m Arkansas, and between 25 and 30 years of age,—the precise cause of the quarrel is not known.

Oct. 31. To-day we lay over to rest ourselves and animals and afford them an opportunity of feeding on what little grass there is in this place.

November 1st. Crossed two branches of the Gila, and finding no pasturage fed the animals on cane and willow. I had the good fortune to kill five partridges at three shots, which furnished us with an excellent dish.

During the seven following days, in which we made about sixty miles, nothing of importance transpired, our route laying for the most part through sandy roads.

Nov. 9th. Remained in camp till noon in order to rest ourselves and animals. There are drifts of sand to the North thick as a snow drift. I have just returned from the river, and have had a refreshing bath in the cool water of the Gila. As we were preparing to start this afternoon, we discovered that five of our animals were missing. We found them about four miles back in a cane thicket. This delaying us some time, we lay over till morning.

Nov. 10th. To-day we pursued our route which lay along the windings of the Gila, the waters of which empty into the Colorado. Throughout this tract of country the mountain presents one unbroken chain of rugged rocks, piled up in wild confusion, their lofty summits seeming to pierce the clouds. We halted during the night in the cannon of the mountains.

Sunday, Nov. 11th. We pursued our journey over a hard sandy road through a wilderness of sun flowers. We halted for the night at about two miles distant from the Colorado, without fire, wood or fodder. Our camp was not inappropriately termed " Camp starvation. " We had made sixteen miles.

Nov. 12th. Arrived at the river, we found about thirty American soldiers stationed, who had a ferry over which they transported emigrants at the following rates :—Waggons $4, mules $1, and men $4. The river here is one hundred and seventy yards in breadth, with a current of about $3\frac{1}{2}$ miles an hour. It is crossed by means of a rope suspended from either bank,—a mode of travel very disagreeable and somewhat dangerous. Capt. Thorn, of Col. Colier's party on endeavoring to pass here on the 28th October, on two log canoes lashed together, was upset, and, together with three others, swept down on the current and drowned. His body was found about six miles below this spot, and was interred here. There has a team arrived to-day from San Diego to carry his remains to the States. The Gila empties into the Colorado about one-half a mile above the ferry, nearly at right angles, and just below the place of disembougement, is a gorge of rocks and sand, which imparts a somewhat picturesque appearance to the spot. On the top of this the Topographical Engineer has his department, and just below the Lieutenant and Commisary have their quarters. We crossed the river in safety and encamped about two miles from the opposite bank.

Nov. 13th. We laid in camp in order to collect musketi beans to supply our animals while crossing the Desert, we obtained about six bushels and cut a quantity of cane. While engaged in this it rained heavily, which made the mud stick to our feet like snow shoes.

Nov. 4th. We started at 6 o'clock, and proceeded along a sandy road skirting the Colorado. Towards nightfall we passed through an Indian village, and after crossing the river in the spot crossed by Col. Cook, camped, without grass.

The following day we held on the same course, and made about fourteen miles.

Nov. 16th. Started at 5½ o'clock in the morning. As we ascended towards the table land, the weather was fine and cool, but on the top nothing met the eye but one arid waste of sand, into which our rolling wagon sunk four or five inches above the felloes. The sand continued to drift badly all day, and on camping at seven in the evening, (during which time we had halted three times,) the mules were nearly exhausted. Securing them to the wheels, we gave them a small quantity of corn, and stretched ourselves to slumber on the sandy desert of California, the constant braying of the mules for water during the night, being our serenade. This day we accomplished nineteen miles.

Nov. 17th. Drove until we reached the second well of Cook's, where we stopped to breakfast. The well was dry, but we shortly sunk one and procured a quantity of water sufficient to afford considerable relief to our mules. After moving on about three miles farther we came to a Lagoon, where we found plenty of water. During the afternoon the road became somewhat less barren, with some signs of herbage and at 7 P. M. we came to New River, or Camp Salvation, where we found several companies encamped.

Sunday, 18th. Have decided on remaining here two or three days, in order that our travel-jaded mules may recruit themselves on the good pasturage.

Nov. 19th. Business of the day, pulling and curing grass, wherewith to supply the mules while traversing the remainder of the Desert. Mr. John Carey came into our camp last evening, who informed us of the destruction of the Empire steamboat. We purpose going to-morrow.

November 20th. The weather clear and fine—are employed in making and twisting hay and preparing for the afternoon's departure. Several men have dropped in our camp here, who, abandoning their teams, have taken to foot travel.

At 1 o'clock we drove on to a Lagoon, and halted to rest the mules and take tea. The road now is very good. Started again this evening and camped at another Lagoon, having made fifteen miles.

Nov. 21st. This morning we were aroused by the enlivening sound of the Bugle and Drum. Being so late when we arrived at camp, we had failed to perceive them till their music discovered them to us at day-dawn. They were Mexican soldiers going to determine the boundary betwixt that country and the United States. They presented a somewhat curious spectacle, being mounted on mules and jacks, with several females in company.

November 22d. Started this morning at six o'clock—the wind blowing strongly and somewhat cold. Our route lies over rolling sand banks, whose every varying surface still presents one aspect of unchanging barrenness. Not a tiny shrub or blade of grass is visible. On either side of us piled one upon another in rugged grandeur, are lofty hills, whose bleak summits wear the same aspect of desolation. On some of these we discovered vast quantities of shells, which would seem to justify the idea, that the salt waves of the ocean must have rolled its mighty tide over this arid soil. Towards noon we arrived at Caresso, or Cane creek, the first water that emigrants find for upwards of ninety miles. In the afternoon we started in the bed of the Creek, the sand deep, and the wind blowing with great violence, which rendered our traveling very difficult and tardy. We held on until evening and halted at the base of the mountain for the night, having accomplished about seventeen miles.

Nov. 23d. The weather cold, and gusty, and the sand covering our loads as if it were snow. We halted at noon and found water and grass at a spot called Vallietto. The grass is impregnated with salt and the water with sulphur.

Nov. 24th. The weather this morning is clear and exceedingly cold, last night being the coldest we have yet had. The ice is rather thick, and the sky begins to assume the aspect of winter. Passsng over rocks and high mountain we discovered in our descent a sulphur spring, when we halted for noon. Here we saw a number of Indians, but could not ascertain to what tribe they belonged. After proceeding over a sandy track, in the afternoon, having made about four miles, we entered a ravine, or cannon, in the mountains which was so narrow that it would barely admit our wagon,—traveling in this manner for a considerable time, the rocks impending over our heads in many instances for several feet, we emerged about sundown on the open mountain, in order to ascend which we were obliged, all hands, to put our shoulders alternately at the wheel, and sometimes it required our united efforts to start the team when it once became stationary. This is the spot where Col. Cook cut through the rock to make a way for his teams and repacked his wagons. It is the most hideous road I ever saw. We made to-day about ten miles.

Sunday, 26th. The road to-day has been pretty good, and about one o'clock we arrived at the valley of San Fillipy.— Here we halted to feed our animals on the salt grass, which is abundant, and to prepare dinner for ourselves. There are a few Indian huts in this vicinity and some lodges. To what tribe they belong we could not discover. They subsist principally on a species of nut which grows here in abundance. We remained at San Fillipy during the 26th in order to recruit our mules.

Nov. 27th. Travelling eight miles we arrived at Oak Grove, where we halted till noon, and then resuming our route, traversed a high hill sprinkled with small oaks. On ascending we emerged into a valley, where we discovered a man plowing, from whom we ascertained that it was Mr. Warner's Ranche. We halted for the night.

Nov. 28th. Rained until two o'clock. At about a distance

of a mile from this morning's starting point we came to a road forking off in two directions. At the junction of these diverging roads, one of which conducts to Los Angel and the other to San Diego ; stands Mr. Warner's Ranche and stone house, at which provisions may be obtained at high rates.—Flour at three shillings a pound, whiskey two shillings a glass, &c., &c. We pushed on over the San Diego road, where we passed several Indian Lodges, and arrived at San Isabelle.— This is a Mexican Ranche and contains several thatched lodges. The people pay little attention to the cu tivation of land, but raise excellent cattle. We met occasionally, however, with a well cultivvaed valley.

Nov. 29th. Weather rather milder. The road steep and country mountainous. Halting at noon in a valley we met with a Mr. Williams, the owner of a ranche a short distance from this spot, who is from the Gold M.nes and relates marvelous stories of them. He is from San Diego and gave us all requisite information respecting the route, price of shipping &c. Passing on in the afternoon we came up with another Mexican Ranche plentifully stocked with cattle. Some of our company purchased a quarter of beef for twelve shillings. We drove until evening and camped at the foot of a very high mountain for the night.

Nov. 30th. Continued our route over mountain and through valley gorge, across high hills and plains which, seemed almost interminable, and halted at noon, our animals being very tired, and a high mountain being before us. In the afternoon we began to ascend, which could only be affected by one of us lifting at each wheel and pushing from behind the vehicle.— At last, in a state bordering on exhaustion, we attained the summit of the mountain, and the view which greeted us was most beautiful. Away over the barren waste, shone the blue waves of the vast Pacific sleeping calmly in the light of the fast fading day, and as the breeze fanned our brow we could well fancy that we were inhaling the pure ocean air. We prepared to descend the mountain, and found the road (if road it can be called indeed) most terrible. It was with the utmost difficulty that we could prevent the wagon from pitching down headlong. After reaching the valley we came in sight of a Ranche and camped for the night. This day we made sixteen miles and is one of the hardest ones we have yet had.

Dec. 1st. About noon to-day we came in sight of the Mission of San Diego. We drove until we neared the Ranche and halted in the valley till morning.

Sunday, Dec. 2d. Visited the San Diego Mission. It was deserted not long since by the Spaniards or Mexicans and is now used as a Ranche. The main building is from two to three hundred feet in length and faces to the West. On the North corner is the church, in which are placed several images and paintings. One of the latter, representing the "Resurrection," is very finely executed. There are a number of lesser buildings. In the centre of the Ranche is a spacious yard. The main building faces two extensive Olive yards, or orchards, beautifully laden with delicious fruit, while rising at intervals above the Olive trees, towers a stately palm. In the yard stands a press for straining the oil from the olive, with a kettle constructed for aiding in its preparation. They have three spacious cisterns, or reservoirs, which are capable of containing a large quantity of water. To the rear lies a large vineyard well stocked with prime grapes.

The Mission is oocupied by two familles from Wisconsin, some California Emirants and two soldiers. The whole presents a highly pleasing and picturesque appearance.

Monday, 3d. We started for the town of San Diego to sell our mules and prepare for shipping the first opportunity. After a drive of six miles we arrived at the town, but the offers for our mules were so inconsiderable that we resolved to fill our water vessels and drive down to the beach, which we accordingly did and camped for the night.

Dec. 4th. The weather is cloudy and indicates rain. The rainy season may be said to have commenced. Vandercook and McDonell went to town to-day and sold the mules for one hundred dollars. The town is small but is about the best looking one we have seen. There are two companies of soldiers quarted here and one at the Beach. The Bay, though small, presents a noble appearance. There is one vessel now in port, arrived from San Francisco, and bound to Boston with hides, with which she is being laden. She will carry about ninety thousand. We are waiting most anxiously for the first appearance of a vessel. Provisions here are exceedingly high —Flour $40 per barrel, or 25 cents per pound, Ham $1 per pound, Whiskey 25 cents a glass, Crackers 25 cents per pound, Sugar $37\frac{1}{2}$ cents, and not half enough at this price to victual one half the population. There is a heavy duty imposed on

Ducks, Geese, and all kinds of game. Mechanics make very good wages; Carpenters $3 and half ration a day, and common laborers $75 a month. There is one building here at the beach in process of erection which is, with the exception of three or four stores for hides, the only one. The soldiers are quartered in tents.

Dec. 5th. Rested the greater part of the day, it being very rainy. Robert has gone to town to get a small supply of beans, while we remain in this place of land sharks. There has been a death on board the ship lying here, to-day.

Dec. 6th. The weather cold, and the mountains to the northward covered with snow. This morning three of us boys let ourselves out to load coal on board the steamship Unicorn, at $4 a day and found, which is the first day's *paid* work we have done since we started. We dined with the ships crew, and commenced working again in the evening at $1 an hour, worked three hours, and having took tea, received $7 for the day's work. One soldier died to day at his tent.

Dec. 7th. The steamer cleared to-day about three P. M. and some of our company forwarded letters by a Boston gentleman, to their friends. We have been shown a number of samples of gold in rocks and dust, hear many a " tall" story concerning the diggings. One young man who has been conveyed ashore from the steamer, lies at the point of death, and here without a friend to soothe or comfort him—to administer consolation or to whisper hope—here he has been laid down to die, " a stranger in a strange land" with but a hired attendat to watch him in his last moments.

Dec. 8th. Weather clear and cold, another death on board the ship.

Dec. 9 and 10. At town purchasing provisions, there being no vessel in sight.

Dec. 11th. Occupied to day in baking Johnny cakes, and cooking clams of which we caught a large supply yesterday. The wolves by night and day are our constant companions, and sometimes we are so disturbed by their long, dreary howl through the night that we have to rise and drive them off.

Dec. 12. To day I went to San Diego to witness one of the favorite sports common to this country and old Spain, a "Bull Fight." The scene commenced in the main Plaza, between one of these animals and twelve Castilians. The Bull was brought into the ring with a rope attached to his horns and hinder hoof. He was then thrown down and the rope from the horns cast off, while the animal was enraged by having blankets shook at him. When sufficiently excited he was loosed. and he immediately charged upon his prosecuters, thrusting his horns through several of the horces. I saw nothing, however, that pleased me in the spectacle, excespt the splendid horsemanship of the riders. Their skill in throwing the lance is admirable. The spectators appeared to be all highly delighted.

Dec. 13th. Emigrants are daily arriving here. To-day I killed a rabit and discovered my jack knife which I had lost the previous day, an article not so unimportant as it might appear to be at first mention. Another soldier has died, to-day, making the fifth since our arrival here.

From this date until the 17th little of consequence has occcurred. During the night of the 17th, however, a severe storm raged, with incessant and tremendous rain.

Dec. 18th. This morning the beach presents rather a poor appearance. Half of the emigrant's tents, that numbered some hundreds, are blown down, and the majority of the occupants drenched to the skin.

Dec. 19th. All occupied in rearing tents, drying tent cloth and bedding and keeping a sharp look out for the steamer which is now due.

From the 19th until this time, (the 25th) we have been looking out anxiously for the steamer but without encouragement. To-day we took dinner with Mr. Curtis, when we had fish and pie for the first time since we left the States; and the steamer California touched here on her way to San Francisco, with a full compliment of passengers. The Captain consented to take us on board, if we could obtain the request of the passengers. Accordingly we got up a paper, signed by all our company and others, but it did not succeed as readily as we hoped. He said that he would stay until the next day noon, and we retired.

The next day we were on board the steamer early, but her steam was up, and she soon moved off, and many a face betokened bitter disappointment as she swept away from view, our own among the rest; our application being unsuccessful. As soon as she had left, we hastened to see the captain of the Belfast and procure passage, which we could barely get, as there was a great rush, and the brig could not accumodate more than sixty or seventy passengers. We paid $35 and furnished ourselves withe everything except wood and water. To-day I fell in with Mr. McCoy of Albany, (formerly Waterford,) who shipped on the 13th of November from New York, and was now on his way San to Francisco.

Dec. 27th. The weather, cold and damp—many complaining of cold and sore throats, myself being one of the number.

Dec. 28th. Purchased a supply of Government provisions to carry on ship board.

Early on the morning of the 29th we got all the baggage on board, except our bedding, which would have to press the beach of San Diego once more, before we bade adieu to the white tent with which it is covered.

Dec. 29th. To-day about noon we shipped on board the Brig Belfast, of Belfast, Maine—Jordan, Master. She carried in all about 80 passengers, the whole of whom were heartily sea sick before night.

Dec. 30th. Out of sight of land, except one of the San Padro Islands—made a southerly direction during the day, but progressed very slowly.

Dec. 31st. Gala sprung up and a heavy sea, but the vessel now made on in her right course, about north west. All were pretty sick, and I myself suffered severely from a bad head-ache.

Jan. 1st, 1950. Was awoke this morning by the sailors wishing each other a happy New Year,—there is heavy sea, and the wind south east.

2d. Cloudy with frequent squalls, the wind favorable, and a rather heavy sea, the ship rolling frequently so heavy as to dip her trysails in the water. Her sails are all set and she glides smoothly onward. There is considerable excitement here in watching the whales which are sporting around us, and making the arch like jets of water propelled from their nostrils to a height of thirty feet. My head pains me exceedingly, and I am not able to enjoy the excitement.

Jan. 3rd. The wind about two o'clock this morning sprung up afresh from the North East and we were obliged to beat. We saw an English Vessel to-day and exchanged signals.— We caught glimpses this morning of land near Monterey.— Gale continued with a heavy sea when they subsided.

Jan. 4th. Eearly this morning we had a fair view of land well timbered and mountainous. On taking observation the

Capt. found that we had run some distance past the Bay. We then put about on a south east course, keeping close on the wind until eleven A. M., and then changing our tack, stood towards the Bay. A heavy fog now sprung up, which compelled us to put to sea for the night.

Jan. 5th. No land visible in any direction—little wind—cloudy, and in doubt about the direction of the harbor.

Jan. 6th. Wind blowing from the shore directly in our teeth. Every thing just now seems unpropitious.

7th. Fog increases and gale becomes more violent.

8th. The storm is at its height—fog dense as night—the sea breaking heavily over the vessel—cooking suspended, and all compelled to fast. Each man's countenance is gloomy and his spirits dejected—the officers make preparation for a severe night, and all sails are reefed, save the foresail and main top.

9th. Storm abates—cooking operations resumed. Slapjacks are in great demand, but the weather is too hazy to admit of taking any observations—no land visible.

10th. Weather a little clearer. Our first mate hailed the bark Bostonia, commanded by Captain Garner, from whom he received some valuable information touching our latitude &c. Our Captain invited him on board, on which he came in company with the physician and several others.

Jan. 11. Morning clear--the islands which we had seen on the 5th are again visible, and matters look a little more encouraging. At 9 o'clock a light breeze sprung up which was favorable for making port, and we are now sweeping along in full sail. Several vessels are in sight. At 5 P. M. we entered the Bay, which presented a magnificent appearance—the hills along the shore begin to wear a verdant color and give signs of returning spring. At 8 P. M. We dropped anchor, and turned into our berths and slept soundly for the first time in two weeks.

Jan 12. All hands are up before breakfast, and busy in cooking, after which we commenced taking our baggage ashore. This done we, we pitched our tents some ten or fifteen rods from the margin of the beach and suspended our toil for some time.

Jan. 13th. To-day we have had the pleasure of meeting several acquaintances from the States, who told us that they were surprised to see us, as report had said that we had returned to the States or had got scalped by the Indians. From this date, to the 5th of Feb., we remained knocking around, when R. Blake and myself were employed by Mr. N—, to set out on a hunting excursion.

Feb. 6th. We commenced preparations for the mines—to this end, a whale boat was purchased, with full rigging, for $350, which was deemed the most advisable mode of reaching Yubaville on Yuba river. Having purchased provisions and other necessaries, we started from San Francisco at 12 M.; our crew six in number. We arrived at Dugal Island at two P. M.; wind and tide both being unfavorable, which made rowing no child's play. At 5 P. M., we moored our boat and camped on the north west side of the Bay for the night.

Feb. 7th. We got under weigh about 7 A. M., having the tide in our favor. We passed Round Island and the two Sister Islands, and shot into San Pueblo Bay. The tide now set against us, and we put ashore on the S. E. side and got dinner. During this operation the tide had left our boat high and dry, which detained us until 7 P. M,—the time did not drag heavily, as the romantic scenery around this spot might well help to wile away alonger time. On the return of the tide we started, not considering our mooring safe. After seering for some time, we observed a lifght on the shore, and making for it, discovered that it proceeded from an encampment. We accordingly landed, pitched our tent, and cooked supper.

Fed. 8th. Morning, clear and cold. Started at seven A. M., and shortly afterwars entered Benitee Straits. which brought us in sight of Benicia city, situate on the N. W. side. Two vessels lying here at anchor, one a war sloop and the other a frigate—the latter has a band on board, and we heard them playing up " Hail Columbia" in grand style. Nothing could have impressed me more feelingly than the thoughts which were called up by this old familiar strain. About ten we entered Suisam Bay, when the wind for the first time became favorable. While the breeze lasted we shipped our oars and ate dinner. Shortly after the wind died away, and again we had to bend to our oars. As we moved up the Bay the Sierra Nevada Mountains rose in sight.

10th. Rowed all day, and camped at night, and were much annoyed by mosquitoes.

Feb. 11. Weather pleasnt as usual. Shortly after starting we entered the Slue, which cuts off some miles, but the current runs at the rate of five miles an hour, in order to avoid which, we were obliged to keep changing from side to side. At noon we entered the main channel of the river.

Feb. 13. Got off at eight and soon after arrived in the city. It was just after the deluge and many of the houses were half covered with water. It is commodiously situated on the east side of the river, on a level plain, on the junction of the Sacramento and American. We made our purchases, and returned, taking with us a Mr. McFarland, an acquaintance from Lansingburgh.

Feb. 14th. Passed on up the river—saw two saw mills, one of which was worked by steam, and the other by oxen.— The banks here are well timbered with heavy oak. In the afternoon we arrived at Fremont and entered Feater river, and on camping shot some fine partridges.

Feb. 15. We were visited to-day by an old Kentucky emigrant, who made application for Whiskey,—started at 7 o'clock and shortly overhauled a small steam Boat, we rowed past her, and beat her one mile in six. We stopped at Nicholas Ranche about 10 and delayed until the steamer came up. The passengers wanted us to take them in tow. At 11½ o'clock, we passed the mouth of Bear river, and the residence of Capt. Sutter, and at 5 P. M. camped on the east side of the river.

15th. Clear and mild. After some heavy tugging against the current, we arrived at Yuba city at 10. We pushed on up the river until eleven—pitched our tent—unloaded our boat, and found several men going to the mines. Drinking and gambling are much practiced here.

17th. This morning, Mr. McL. and myself went off on an exploring expedition.

HOMEWARD ROUTE.

November 25th. Started this day from "Rough & Ready" about 1 oclock, in company with O'Connor, McDonnell, and H Vandercook. The two former returned after accompanying us three miles. After proceeding about twelve miles farther, we stopped for the night at Berry's Ranche.

Nov. 26th. Started after breakfast and about 11 A. M. reached Long Bar, where we met with Mr. Swartout, who was well. At evening we reached Marysville, where we saw Pierce, Donbridge, and Nobles, and staid over night.

Nov. 27th. This day Robert and I separated, taking leave of each other on the boat, *he* returning to the mines and *I* proceeding to Sacramento. Here 1 stopped over night and saw James Lansing, Doctor Salter, Colvers, and Hanford.

Nov. 28th. Remained here awaiting the boat.

29th. Secured a ticket for a passage to Panama on board the "Republic." 1 then went to the Post Office, and saw Mr. Skillman, of Troy, on my way there,—went down to Long Wharf to see Mr. Pratt, found him, and he accompanied me on board the steamer. There I met with *Mr. Wheeler* and *Mr. Hawkins,* and Doct. Treist. The boat soon got her steam up—the ropes were cast off—the water whitened into foam as her revolving paddles dipped into the wave—the hurrah's died away in the distance and ere long the waving of hats from the assembled crowd on shore was undiscernable in the deepening twilight.

Nov. 30th. Wind blowing from the Northwest, causing a rough sea—sea sickness prevailing.

December 1st. Wind continues to blow strongly from the

Northwest, accompanied by a high sea. Saw an immense whale. The passengers this day were sorted into messes, of about seventy or eighty to a mess.

Dec. 2d. Vessel moving in a Southeasterly direction, under fore and foretop sail. Islands visible to the Northeast.

Dec. 3d. Heavy sea and high wind—mountains faintly visible to leeward—latitude 27 3, longitude 115 08—distance accomplished during the last 24 hours 219 miles.

Dec. 4th. Made 112 miles.

Dec. 5th. Crowded on all sail—passed Cape St. Lucas and made 270 miles.

Dec 6th. Weather fine and warm—all sail set—latitude 14 W., longitude 107 N.—Number of miles made 190. There was a disturbance to-day, occasioned by a quarrel between a Southerner (a gambler) and one of the colored cooks, the result of which terminated in the Southern gentleman being put into confinement.

Dec 7th. Came within sight of the two highest mountains in Mexico (volcanic). Discovered two sails—the one to the windward, a brig, and a barque to leeward.

Sunday, Dec. 8th. Arrived this day at the entrance of Acapulca Bay, and hove to until this morning.

Dec. 9th. Took a good bath in the ocean, and then visited the town. There are about two thousand inhabitants, the greater number of whom divide their time between cock fighting and fandangos. Every variety of tropical fruit is here in great abundance.

Dec. 10th. Occupied by the ships crew in taking in water.

11 and 12th. Sea somewhat rough, and sickness prevailing among the passengers.

13th. Wind ahead—squally, with rough sea.

14th. Lost one of the cabin passengers overboard—merely a hog, however, from the fore cabin.

15th and 16th. Wind continues ahead, sea boisterous.

17th. Passed a ship freighted with mules, bound for Valparaiso. Held an indignation meeting, and issued a protest on the score of scantiness of provisions.

18th. Entered the Bay of Panama, and on rounding the point, passed the steamship "Antelope" bound for San Francisco.

19th. Arrived at the harbor at 2 o'clock P. M. and were taken ashore in a boat manned by natives who charged us $2.

Dec. 20th. I spent this day in inspecting the town and suburbs. The houses are built principally of stone, and are from two to three stories in height. There are several churches here, and a nunnery. The town is surrounded by a large and expensive wall, erected as a fortification. Disposed upon it, at stated distances, are six large brass cannon. Just on the outskirts of the town is the hill whereon Bolivar planted his cannon, surrendering after firing but three shots.

Dec. 21st. Hired an *"umbra"* to take my baggage to Cruses, for which I paid $4. Started about nine A. M. over a road, built about one hundred and fifty years ago,·and which I should judge has never been repaired since. My *"umbra"* tiring, I stopped for the night at a native ranch, where I procured an egg, a small piece of meet and some coffee.

22d. This morning we started early. The road is very rocky and the general aspect of the surrounding scenery highly picturesque. The country is well timbered, and vines flourish with great luxurance. The sharp quick cry of the parrots and the chattering and jabbering of the monkies, are incessant as we travel onward. We arrived at Cruses about two o'clock this afternoon.

The town of Cruses stands on the eastern side of the Chagres river, and is distant about thirty miles from Panama.— The inhabitants are chiefly natives. The buildings principally consist of cane, roofed with reeds.

We started down the river in a boat plied by two natives, and towards evening arrived at Gorgona, where we halted for the night.

Dec. 23d. Arrived at Chagres about 12 P. M. and got a thorough drenching from a violent shower before we succeeded in getting under shelter. Here we found about two thousand passengers awaiting an opportunity to return to the States.

The diary is here brought to an abrupt conclusion.

While at Chagres Mr. ALDRICH was attacked by a prevailing malady,prostrating both mind and body, and incapacitating him from continuing the narrative.

During his homeward passage from Panama the disease exhibited yet more alarming symptoms, and when he once more returned to his friends, it was only in time to receive at their hands the last sad rite of burial.

The unfinished Journal is, however, submitted to the perusal of his friends, in the belief that they will discover in it much of interest, notwithstanding the unfinished and hasty manner in which it has been written, and the occurrences of chasms which the narrator himself alone could fittingly supply.